GOLD AND GLORY
THE ROAD TO
EL DORADO

Text by Ellen Weiss

Paintings by Robert Krogle

Pencils by Larry Navarro
with Jose Cánovas and Carlos Grangel

Backgrounds by DreamWorks Animation artists.

Art Direction and Design by Paul Elliott

Digital Composition by Dan Hosek

Special thanks to Bonne Radford for her time and generosity.

Published by Dutton Children's Books,
a division of Penguin Putnam Books for Young Readers,
345 Hudson Street, New York, New York 10014

Printed in USA
CIP Data is available.
ISBN 0-525-46306-2
First Edition
1 3 5 7 9 10 8 6 4 2

THE ROAD TO EL DORADO

WANTED

REWARD
100 DOUBLOONS.

Text by Ellen Weiss
Paintings by Robert Krogle

Deep in the emerald green jungle, hidden behind a towering waterfall, there lay a magical, golden city—El Dorado, the land of the Eagle and the Jaguar. For a thousand years, the gods had blessed the city with peace and happiness.

But today that happiness was threatened, for something terrible and mysterious had happened. In the middle of the day, the sun had been blotted out, and the world was plunged into darkness. What could it mean?

The mighty Tzekel-Kan, high priest of the Jaguar, had an answer.

"The gods are coming!" Tzekel-Kan proclaimed. "They will cleanse this city—with blood! And sacrifice!" Two citizens, a man and a beautiful young woman, were brought forward, bound and struggling.

"Stop!" cried the good-hearted Chief Tannabok. "We do not know that the gods will demand sacrifice."

But Tzekel-Kan had been waiting a long time for this moment. It was just as his codex—his religious text—had described. "The age of the Jaguar is upon us! The omens are clear!" spat the priest. "Do not doubt the prophecies!"

"I don't," the Chief answered. "I doubt *you*. If the gods have a problem with my people, then let them appear and speak for themselves."

"And so they shall. I, Tzekel-Kan," he said, "summon the gods to El Dorado!"

At that very moment, on a dock half a world away in Spain, a game of dice was going on.

"Seven!" crowed one of the players, a tall, dark fellow. This was Tulio.

"All right, partner!" cried his friend Miguel. They were winning big—which was not amazing, considering that they cheated.

It was a good day for Tulio and Miguel to find willing victims. The waterfront was crawling with sailors, for the fearsome explorer Cortes was about to sail for the New World. Astride his magnificent stallion, Altivo, Cortes was supervising the loading of his ships. "Today we sail to conquer the New World!" he said. "For Spain! For glory! For gold!" His cruel face showed that he was a man who always got what he wanted.

Meanwhile, the unfortunate sailor was not done losing. He was out of money, but he wanted to roll the dice again. "I've got this!" he offered, taking a rolled-up parchment from his doublet. "A map of the wonders of the New World!"

Tulio was interested only in winning money or gold. But Miguel was excited. For while Tulio was forever scheming, Miguel was forever dreaming.

"Tulio, look!" he pleaded. "El Dorado, the city of gold! Imagine the glory! This could be our fate!"

"If I believed in fate," whispered Tulio, "I wouldn't be playing with loaded dice."

But Miguel talked Tulio into it, as usual. Before Tulio rolled the dice, though, the sailor interrupted. "This time," said the sailor, "we use mine."

Even though Tulio didn't believe in fate, it seemed that fate believed in Tulio. One roll of the new dice, and, surprise of surprises, the map was his.

But now the sailor examined Tulio's old dice. He was on to the scam. "Your dice are loaded!" he screamed.

Tulio immediately turned on Miguel, deeply offended. "You gave me loaded dice?" he said. He began walking away, only to find that he had run smack into a Spanish constable. And the constable, sad to say, was not part of the act.

"Guard, arrest him!" demanded Tulio, thinking fast.

"*He* was the one who was cheating! Arrest *him!*" ordered Miguel.

"*En garde!*" Tulio challenged Miguel as the crowd looked on, horrified.

"*En garde* yourself! I will give you the honor of a quick and painless death!"

"You fight like my sister!" Miguel taunted as they crossed swords.

"I've fought your sister—that's a compliment!"

Miguel and Tulio were having fun, but it was time to wrap up the performance. "Ladies and gentlemen, we've decided it's a draw!" Tulio announced. "Thank you for coming!"

They leaped over a wall, laughing as they tossed aside their swords. But there was one small problem they hadn't counted on, and it looked a lot like a bull. They had leaped right into a bullpen.

They vaulted over the side of the pen, but the bull crashed through the gate and thundered after them. They raced through the streets, the bull and several constables at their heels. Swinging on a clothesline, they landed on a rooftop.

Now they were cornered—or were they? What was that down below on the dock? Aha—just the thing! Barrels!

"I'll bet we can make that!" shouted Miguel.

"Two pesetas says we can't!"

"You're on!"

As they landed in the barrels, Tulio tossed the bet money into Miguel's barrel. They were safe!

Or maybe not. A little later, they felt an odd sensation of being hauled up into the air. That was because they *were* being hauled up into the air. The barrels were being loaded onto Cortes's ship. "Okay, we gotta move fast," said Tulio. "On three, we jump out. One...two...three!" they said as, unbeknownst to them, a heavy trunk was loaded on top of the barrels.

"One...two...three!" they were still saying later. Then their problem was solved. The barrels were opened. But now they had a new problem: Cortes.

"You will be flogged," thundered Cortes, "and you will work on the sugar plantations in Cuba for the rest of your miserable lives!"

Their next stop was the brig. Tulio thought hard about how they were going to escape. To help himself think, he banged his head against the wall.

On the deck above them, Altivo, Cortes's giant war horse, was being groomed. A sailor walked past him with a basket of apples. Altivo was a picky eater: he always picked eating. He wanted an apple. Badly.

An apple dropped from the basket, right into the brig. "Hey, Altivo!" called Miguel, holding it up. "You want the nice apple? Find me a pry bar!"

"He can't understand that," said Tulio.

Tulio was right. Altivo didn't bring a pry bar. He brought the keys instead.

They were out! "Thank you, Altivo!" said Miguel.

They sneaked to a longboat to make their escape—but there was a problem. Altivo was following them. He still wanted that apple.

"Fetch!" said Tulio as he threw the apple to Altivo.

Oops. The apple bounced twice off the ship and flew over the side. Altivo flew right after it. Now they were all in the water.

And they were all in big trouble. Boring down on them was the next galleon in Cortes's fleet! It almost drowned them in a wave that flipped their longboat and flung most of their food into the sea.

Altivo flailed the water with his hooves. "Loop the rope under the horse!" yelled Tulio, climbing onto the upside-down boat and tying the rope to the tiller.

A little later, they looked around. Phew. The ship hadn't squished them. The boat was right side up, and Tulio, Miguel, and Altivo were sitting in it.

"Did any of the supplies make it?" Tulio asked.

"Well, um, yes and no," Miguel replied, pointing to Altivo, whose cheeks were stuffed with the last of their food. At least he looked guilty.

Things went downhill from there.

A storm came up, tossed the boat, and left the adventurers wretched. There would be no gold for Tulio, no glory for Miguel.

"Tulio," Miguel said solemnly, "did you ever imagine it would end like this?"

"The horse is a surprise," said Tulio. "But if it's any consolation, Miguel, you made my life an adventure."

"You made my life rich," sobbed Miguel.

The horse just rolled his eyes.

But, just when things looked bleakest…"Laaaaaand!"

They had washed up on a beautiful beach…with beautiful sand…and a beautiful…*skull*?

"Let's leave!" said Tulio.

But Miguel had other ideas. "Tulio!" he said. "We've done it! It's all right here! The whistling rock…the stream…the mountains—it is! It's all on our map to El Dorado!"

"You still have the *map?*" said Tulio disgustedly. "You kept the map, but you couldn't grab a little more food? I wouldn't set foot in that jungle for a million pesetas."

"How about a hundred million? El Dorado is the city of gold. You know, dust, nuggets, bricks, a temple of gold…but you don't want to go. So let's row back to Spain."

"Wait…wait a minute. New plan. We find the city of gold, we take the gold—and then we go back to Spain," said Tulio.

"And buy Spain!" Miguel chimed in.

The only one who didn't look excited was Altivo. Maybe these two guys weren't smart enough to be scared, but the horse certainly was.

"Come on, Tulio," said Miguel. "Let's follow that trail!"

"What trail?" asked Tulio, looking around and seeing none.

"The trail we blaze!" said Miguel.

So off they set into the New World, with Altivo clomping reluctantly along.

They climbed, they slid, they scrambled through the dark, shadowy green jungle. Along the way, they made a new friend—a little armadillo—and they named him Bibo. They did not, however, make friends with the monkeys who stole their clothing.

Then they fell down a steep ravine. Lights out.

Tulio recovered first. He looked around and saw a waterfall and a great stone...thing. What on earth was it? It matched the last symbol on their map, but it definitely wasn't made of gold.

"Wake up!" Tulio said to Miguel. "We're there."

"But...this...can't..." said Miguel, wondering where the gold was.

"Apparently, *El Dorado* is native for...GREAT...BIG...ROCK!" Tulio taunted. "But I'm feeling generous. I'll give you my share."

"You don't think Cortes could've gotten here before us and..." Miguel wondered.

"And what? Taken all the really BIG rocks? That villain!"

They climbed onto Altivo to leave, and were so busy being miserable that they didn't notice a beautiful girl bursting right through the waterfall. In her arms she concealed a carved, golden head.

She was not alone. Right behind her was a group of soldiers in hot pursuit.

The girl tossed the head to Tulio, and the direction of the soldiers' spears shifted from her to him. Tulio was no fool; he immediately chucked it back to her.

But suddenly, the soldiers stopped. They looked at Tulio and Miguel. Then they looked at the great stone monolith.

Tulio and Miguel looked like the pictures on the monolith—pictures of the gods.

The soldiers grabbed the girl and motioned for Tulio and Miguel to follow them.

With the little armadillo scampering along behind, the soldiers led them past the waterfall and into a tunnel through which a roaring river ran. They boarded a boat, which was then poled through a cavern, then past a pair of gigantic stone pillars, and finally through a great stone gateway and out into the brilliant sunshine of—

"El Dorado!" gasped Miguel and Tulio. They gaped at the incredible splendor of the city before them. The stones glinted in the warm sun, hinting at the gold that lay within the monumental buildings. In fact, many of the buildings were even made of gold.

In the background, they could hear the ominous rumbling of a nearby volcano.

Both the high priest, Tzekel-Kan, and Chief Tannabok were waiting on the great steps of the temple.

"Citizens!" said Tzekel-Kan to the awestruck populace. "Did I not predict that the gods would come to us?"

Miguel and Tulio glanced at each other in confusion. Was this guy talking about them?

As the crowd gasped in fear, the Chief spoke. "My lords, why do you choose to visit us now?"

"You do not question the gods!" bellowed Tzekel-Kan.

"That's right!" agreed Miguel, getting into it. "Do not question us! Or we shall have to unleash our awesome and terrible power!" The volcano rumbled menacingly.

"Excuse us a moment," Tulio said, taking Miguel aside. "You know that little voice people have that tells them to quit when they're ahead?" he whispered. "Well, you don't have one!" He sidestepped the armadillo, who was scurrying around at his feet.

"But they're getting suspicious," said Miguel. "If we don't come up with some kind of megacosmic event—" He bopped Tulio on the forehead to help him think.

"I can't think with all these distractions!" Tulio said, tripping over Bibo again. He looked down, exasperated. "Will you ST-O-P-P-P!?"

Instantly, the volcano was silent.

Miguel and Tulio were just as shocked as the crowd was, but Tzekel-Kan was pleased. These were the gods. His codex was right!

"O mighty lords," said Tzekel-Kan. "Let me show you to your temple." He roughly elbowed the Chief out of his way.

The temple was more luxurious than Tulio and Miguel could ever have imagined. They looked around in amazement. "Tulio, they actually think we're gods!" crowed Miguel.

"It's an entire city of suckers!" Tulio exulted. "We just have to keep this up long enough to load up on the gold and then get out of here!"

Only Altivo noticed the movement behind the potted plant.

"Hello," said the girl they had seen outside the waterfall.

Tulio and Miguel gasped, trying to keep looking godlike.

"Begone!" yelled Miguel in his best godly voice.

"Save it for the high priest, honey," she said. "If you guys want the gold, you're going to need my help."

"What's your angle?" said Tulio. He knew another con artist when he met one.

"You think you're the only ones who dream of better things, of adventure? When you guys are ready to go back to wherever you came from, I'm going with you."

"No, I don't think so," said Tulio.

"Fine. After all, I'm sure you know the proper rituals. Oh, and of course you know all about Xibalba." She turned to leave. "See you at the execution."

"Wait! Hold it," said Tulio.

"Deal?" she said. "Call me Chel. Your new partner."

"That's partner-in-training," said Tulio.

After Chel left, Miguel turned to Tulio. “Maybe they should call this place *Chel*-Dorado.” He chuckled.

“Whoa!” said Tulio. “She’s trouble. Remember the little voice? Imagine that you have one. What would it be saying about Chel?”

“*Rowr!*” said Miguel, thinking about how cute Chel was.

“No! Listen!” said the exasperated Tulio. “*We* are partners. *We* have a plan. And *we* are *pretending* to be gods. Now put Chel in the mix. What is the voice saying?”

“Chel is off-limits?” Miguel guessed.

“Bravo. Chel is off-limits. Shake on it.”

And so it was decided.

Besides, they had a lot to do now. They had to be gods. And it’s tough to be a god.

All that celebrating,

And being adored,

And all that stuff they give you to drink.

The next morning, the gods awoke with a big headache. But it was time to go to the endlessly deep well in the center of the city—the *ceynote*. It was time for Tzekel-Kan's ceremony.

"The city has been granted a great blessing!" proclaimed Tzekel-Kan. "The gods deserve proper tribute!"

That sounded just fine to the gods.

"The dawning of a new age demands...sacrifice!" the priest went on.

As Miguel and Tulio watched in horror, a hapless citizen was dragged to the *ceynote*.

"Stop!" yelled Tulio while he thought of what to say next. "This is not a proper tribute. The, er, stars are not in position for it!"

"Perhaps it is possible that I misread the Heavens?" said the high priest, astounded.

"My lords," said the Chief, stepping forward, "may the people offer you *our* tribute." Piles of gold were being carried out to them.

"Yes, very nice. Lovely," said the gods.

"The gods have chosen!" announced the Chief proudly. "To Xibalba!" The gold bearers began to throw their precious burden down to the spirit world that waited at the bottom of the well.

"No!" yelled Chel, thinking quickly. "The gods wish to bask in the reverence that has been shown them!"

"Stop!" ordered the Chief, smiling just a bit. "They wish to bask!"

Their new partner had saved the day...and the gold!

At that moment, unbeknownst to all, Cortes was landing on the beach. "Well, well," he said, inspecting Miguel's and Tulio's footprints. "What have we here?"

The problem now was how to get the gold back to Spain. They decided to ask the Chief for a big boat. But a big boat, the Chief told them, would take three days to build. Miguel and Tulio agreed to lie low and stay out of trouble as they waited for the boat to be finished.

Miguel stood on the balcony, looking out at the beautiful city.

"It's beautiful, isn't it?" Chel said with a sly little smile. "You know, you really shouldn't miss it."

That was all Miguel needed to hear. In spite of Tulio's strict orders, he could not resist the lure of adventure. In a minute, he was gone.

This left Tulio alone with Chel, which was just the way she wanted it. WIth Chel's help, Tulio was discovering that they shared many interests. Well, two big interests—gold and each other. Tulio could not believe his good fortune. It was always Miguel who had been lucky in love—but here he was with this gorgeous girl!

Meanwhile Miguel and Altivo were exploring the city. It was lovely but empty.

Miguel spotted a guard. "Excuse me," he said. "Where is everybody?"

"They've been cleared from the streets, my lord. The city is being cleansed so that the age of the Jaguar can begin, as you ordered."

That was news to Miguel. As he looked around, he began to notice people hiding, watching him cautiously. This wouldn't do at all.

At Miguel's coaxing, they gradually began to come out. Although they were afraid of their new god, they were also charmed by him. He spotted a child with a ball and invited him to play. Then more children joined in the game, and even the Chief came to watch, smiling.

But trouble was coming down the street: the high priest.

Tzekel-Kan surveyed the scene. Tzekel-Kan was not pleased. "The gods should not be playing ball like this!" he declared.

"*This* is how the gods should play ball!"

Now they were in big trouble. "We're gonna lose!" moaned Tulio, looking around the gigantic stadium.

"Gods don't lose," said Chel as the Chief's humongous warriors jogged out onto the field.

"Play ball!" said Tzekel-Kan. He turned to the gods. "Crush them into the dust," he said. "Enjoy."

The hoop was impossibly high. The opposing team was impossibly good. "This game is impossible!" panted Tulio.

"We need a miracle," said Miguel.

"No, we need to cheat," Tulio gasped.

"New ball!" yelled one of the warriors. This gave Chel an idea.

The new ball was a lot better. It was Bibo, the armadillo.

And finally, with a little bit of last-minute help from Altivo, the game was won. It had been a squeaker, and the gods were battered, but they'd done it!

"Who's the god?" said Miguel jubilantly.

"You the god!" shouted Tulio.

"No, you the god!"

But now Tzekel-Kan was approaching. "You will, of course, wish to have the losing team sacrificed to your glory," he said. The team fell to their knees, stunned.

"Not again," said Miguel. "Look, Tzekel-Kan, forget the sacrifices!"

"Miguel..." said Tulio, trying to shut him up before he got them into more trouble. Why didn't Miguel have a little voice?

"But the sacred writings say how you'll devour the wicked!" said the priest, confused.

"I don't see anyone here who fits that description," said Miguel.

"Well, as Speaker for the Gods, it would be my privilege to point them out."

"The gods are speaking for themselves now!" said Miguel. "These people have no need for you anymore! There will be no sacrifices, not now, not ever! Now get out!"

The crowd burst into cheers. Miguel was immediately picked up and carried off, but not before Tzekel-Kan had noticed a small trickle of blood running down his forehead.

Gods don't bleed, thought the priest. But to Miguel he said, "As...the gods...command."

He would find the answers he needed in his codex. There were dark magics there.

Finally, the boat was finished. Miguel and the Chief sat looking at it. "There's not nearly enough…rope," Miguel said, hoping to delay their departure.

The Chief smiled at his new friend. "You know, Lord Miguel, if you wish to stay, you only need to say so."

"I—I can't," said Miguel sadly. "I have to go back with Tulio. We're partners."

"Well, then…I'd better go get some more rope."

"Oh, Chief, forget about the rope. My mistake."

"To err is human," said the Chief, smiling again.

Miguel smiled, too. He had a feeling that the Chief knew that he and Tulio fell a little short of being gods and that it didn't bother him at all.

Meanwhile, Tulio and Chel were dividing up the gold.

"Half for you and Miguel, half for me," Chel said.

"Ha!" laughed Tulio. "I'll tell you what. I'll let you come back to Spain with us, and—um—you can have ten percent."

"You know, maybe I *won't* go to Spain with you, and take a third."

"Oh," he said, "like you don't want to go to Spain."

"Oh," she returned, "like you don't want me to go to Spain."

"I want you to want…what you want," he finished lamely. "All right. I want you to come to Spain with me and Miguel. Mostly me. Especially me. Only me. Forget Miguel."

They did not notice that Miguel had been watching them from the doorway. He was shocked and angry at the unbelievable words he'd just heard. "Forget Miguel," he said, turning away. "Forget Tulio."

In Tzekel-Kan's temple, the high priest was jubilant. It was time to unleash the Jaguar—time to destroy these phony gods. He'd found just what he needed in his codex.

He took a sip of the thick green brew that bubbled over the fire, and his eyes began to glow. The temple's great stone Jaguar came to life, a creature of darkness and violence. Tzekel-Kan's creature.

The ground shook beneath its feet as the Jaguar destroyed everything that lay in its path. It was looking for the false gods.

"Help us, Lord Miguel!" cried the people. "Save us! Protect us!"

On Altivo's back, Tulio, Miguel, and Chel drew the Jaguar away from the city. It followed and swiped its deadly claw at Altivo, who kicked back at the monster. As its emerald eye shattered, both the Jaguar and Tzekel-Kan howled with pain.

"Altivo," Tulio called, "get Chel out of here!" Then he and Miguel ran, and kept running until they came to—the lava fields!

Crack! The ground suddenly split beneath their feet. Below, bubbling and boiling, they could see the red-hot lava. The Jaguar lunged. But it was too heavy, and it crashed through the earth's crust, plummeting into the molten lava.

"Jump!" cried Tulio to Miguel. They leaped across the chasm as the Jaguar sank out of sight under the lava.

But then, suddenly, the half-melted Jaguar rose up out of the lava and headed straight for them. The Jaguar began slowly herding them onto a narrow ledge above the *ceynote* well, the place of sacrifice! Tzekel-Kan appeared. "I know what you are," he said, "and I know what you are not. And you are not gods!"

Tulio turned to Miguel. "You're not a god?" he said. "You lied to me?"

Miguel fell right into the mock-fight routine. "Hey," he said to the confounded Tzekel-Kan, "it was *his* stupid plan!"

"My plan was that we should lie low! But your plan was to run off and be all 'Look at me! I'm a god!'" yelled Tulio, getting a little too realistic for comfort.

"Well, now you've got all the gold—and Chel! So what do you need me for?" said Miguel.

"Maybe I don't need you anymore!"

"Then why don't you just go back to Spain and I'll stay here?"

Tulio slapped Miguel. Miguel punched Tulio.

"All *riiiiiight!*" they shouted, both turning and knocking down Tzekel-Kan.

"Tie him up!" yelled Tulio. But as they reached for a pair of hanging vines, the Jaguar came barreling down on them.

Now Tulio and Miguel used the vines to swing out of the way. The Jaguar landed astride Tzekel-Kan, and the ledge cracked under its massive weight, sending beast and master hurtling into the well below.

But Tzekel-Kan did not die in the *ceynote* well. He was swept down, down into the river, and then down the waterfall. Now he found himself in a pool of water, cowering at the feet of...Cortes.

The conqueror inspected the priest's golden earring. "Take me to where you got this," he ordered.

Meanwhile, up above, Tulio and Miguel were glad to be alive. "That was good, huh?" said Tulio.

Miguel, however, just glared at him. That argument between them hadn't been just play-acting, and they both knew it.

There was no time to talk about it, though, because the cheering people of El Dorado were approaching. They swarmed around their beloved Lord Miguel, leaving Tulio to be pulled from the ledge by Chel.

"Chief Tanni! I've decided to stay!" Miguel told the Chief.

"Lord Miguel has decided to live among us!" announced the Chief. "What a glorious day for El Dorado!" A great cheer went up.

Tulio was stunned. Was Miguel really serious? But before he could catch Miguel's

eye, Miguel was swept away by the crowd.

It was time for Tulio to go, and Miguel to stay. This was not the way they'd planned things. They'd thought they would always be friends—and partners. Was it all going to end in sadness and bitterness?

Tulio hugged the Chief. Miguel hugged Chel. Tulio hugged Altivo. Then Tulio and Miguel faced each other.

"Well, good luck," said Miguel.

"Yeah, you too," said Tulio. They shook hands, unable to say what was in their hearts. Tulio and Chel got into the boat.

Next to him, Miguel suddenly noticed Altivo prancing nervously and snorting. "What is it, boy?" he asked. Then he saw it. Smoke on the horizon. "Cortes!" he whispered.

A sentry ran in, gasping for breath. "Approaching the city is an army of strangers! And they are being led by Tzekel-Kan!"

"How can we stop them?" said the Chief.

Tulio snapped into action. "Okay," he said. "Here's the gate...and here's the boat..." He set up a cup and a glass to represent them.

"And?" said Chel.

Tulio was stumped. Chel thumped his forehead, but it didn't help.

Then Bibo knocked over the cup, flooding Tulio's "boat." Tulio had the answer.

In moments, the plan was in place. They would topple one of the city's gigantic water cisterns. This in turn would cause a great flood that would send their boat crashing into the stone pillars at the entrance to El Dorado. When they fell, the city would be blocked off from the world forever.

"But...what about the gold?" Chel asked Tulio.

Tulio touched the gold tenderly. Then he snapped to attention once more.

The ropes were rigged, and the cistern began to fall. The boat began to move. But it wasn't moving fast enough. It would be crushed.

"Tulio, the sail!" cried Chel. It was jammed!

Miguel was watching the approaching disaster. "Altivo!" he called.

Miguel jumped on his back, and the horse galloped desperately along the bank above the river.

Tulio saw them from below. "Are you crazy, Miguel?" he shouted.

But Altivo was already leaping from the riverbank, down, down toward the boat. Miguel grabbed the sail and unfurled it. It filled with wind as the cistern toppled and the water began to rise. Man and horse landed perfectly on deck.

"Get off the boat, Miguel, or you'll never see the city again!" yelled Tulio.

"I know! You don't think I'm going to let you have all the fun, do you?"

A great wave caught them, and suddenly they were at the beginning of the tunnel. "We're gonna have to hit the pillars broadside!" yelled Tulio.

"That's your plan? But—the gold!" shouted Miguel.

"I know, I know—just turn the boat!"

They worked furiously to get the boat turned. "On impact, everybody jump!" said Tulio.

They jumped. The great pillars before them shifted, groaned, and gave way. The gold spilled into the water, and so did everyone in the boat, the tunnel collapsing behind them. Tulio had lost his gold, and Miguel had lost his glorious new home. All gone forever.

But they did have one thing left: their friendship.

They all rode the flood out of El Dorado, never to see it again.

Outside the city, Cortes stood looking up at the trickle that was all that remained of the waterfall.

"You lying heathen!" he said to the priest. "There is nothing here." He pushed Tzekel-Kan into the water. "There is no El Dorado," he said. "Onward, men!"

Exhausted and bedraggled, our heroes saw all this from a distance. It was over. They had saved El Dorado.

"Wow," said Miguel. "Now *that* was definitely an adventure."

"Yes, yes, it was...and, um...it was so much gold!" Tulio sobbed. Then he pulled himself together. "I'm fine," he said bravely.

Miguel extended his hand to him. "Partner?" he said.

"Partner," Tulio agreed.

"Hey, guys," called Chel from atop Altivo. "Come on, you don't want to stay here forever, do you?"

"But we don't have a plan," said Tulio.

"That's what makes it interesting!" she said, grinning.

And off they rode into the sunset of the New World—friends for life, come what may. And that was what mattered.

El Do